Nothing More to be Said

Edward L. Hannon

Content

Edward L. Hannon©

Foreword

Existential Reality: Nothing Exists Outside of Containment

Paradoxically, as it relates to the SINGULARITY of Existence, "Containment within containment places all that is seemingly without, to be purely nothing outside of the unique designation of classification-itself. So, the moral of the story is, "Nothing is without classification."

Acknowledgement

I would like to thank "SOURCE CONSCIOUSNESS" for such another profound piece. I would also like to thank those that contributed to Microsoft Clipart and Facebook gifs; which assisted greatly in illustrating my concepts. And Lastly, I would like to thank the dedicated supporter who purchased this 25th publication of mine.

Philosychology

Philosychology (noun) is a study of conscious behavior created by PhTCB (philosopher and teacher of conscious behavior) Edward L. Hannon. This science is a synthesis of empirical psychology along with his philosophies to methodize a practical or practicable solution to resolve the dilemmas, conflicts, or queries that mankind perpetuates upon itself.

Chaplain Edward Lewis Hannon D.D. (Doctor of Divinity)

Always remember that self-confidence can be unfortunately accompanied by the officious opinions of those, who have more than enough advice to give to others; but, have little to offer to their personal state of well-being.

The wise seek to change inwardly; so they accept others as they are. The foolish, being uncomfortable and ignorant of themselves, seek to change the outward appearance of their reality; thus, they project their inner frustrations, by what they expect to vicariously witness in others.

Do not look for life-changing opportunities from those who are barely fit to offer a sensible opinion.

If ever you feel discounted by others, do not hesitate to seek fair winds; in order that you may sail.

Warriors who are committed to upgrade their way of thinking, by way of an initial thought simulation, innately understands that what he/she refuses to virtually consider as a dream (possibility); can become a clear and present nightmare (unfortunate experience) to behold. For it has been said, "If you don't first think it out, you may recklessly act it out."

If you do not have adequate foresight, when dealing with others that are prone to indiscretion, then expect to become reasonably frustrated.

Never trust someone that refuse to live up to the fullness of their personal potential; because they are too busy worrying about what they do not have.

No matter how successful you are or become, do not assume that others will give you the recognition; which you feel that you deserve. Especially, if they have not mutually learned how to hold themselves in favorable regards.

Do not try to hold something that may be beyond reach; by compromising yourself, in order to receive a sense of validation.

Anyone that would ask you to compromise your sense of integrity, in order to suit their exploitive needs, is not worth the effort for further acquaintance.

The Achilles heel of the human species is the frail assumption that it can tame the balance of Nature-Itself; by clinging totally to the disruptive potentials of an exceedingly chaotic disposition.

Foolishness, in youth, can be forgiven; but, foolishness, in old age, can prove to be fatal.

Once you become a skilled and prudent warrior, the only thing that you may need to fear, when facing those willing to restlessly fight themselves into the unfortunate state of self-extinction, is possible boredom from unemployment.

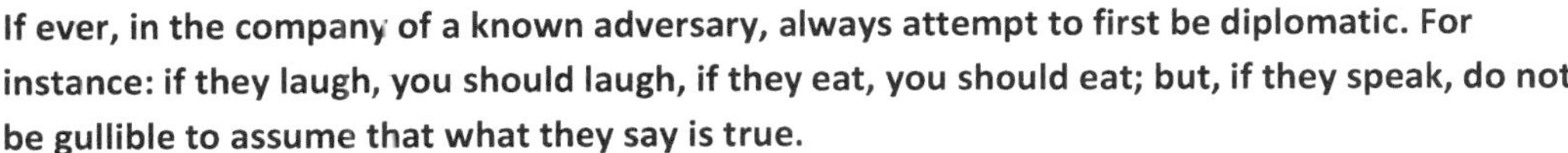

If ever, in the company of a known adversary, always attempt to first be diplomatic. For instance: if they laugh, you should laugh, if they eat, you should eat; but, if they speak, do not be gullible to assume that what they say is true.

Love who You are or where You are from; but not at the unfortunate expense of others.

Do no harm, then you will not have the restlessness of sleep; by worrying about who may be standing over you.

To those who see tomorrow, do not be dismayed; if you are not understood by others that want to remain comfortable, by trying only to seize the day.

I find that, whether subjective or objective, whether sleeping or awakened, whether dark or light and whether it is considered good or evil, Sensation-Itself can be an addiction; by which, we may jeopardize or breach all necessary bounds of reasonableness.

At times, you may find those who do not want to see you happy; because, they are unfortunately disgusted with the sight of themselves.

There are those who respect nothing; not even themselves. So, they have destined themselves to an incorrigible state of personal misery, even unto their final breath. But, I say still be prudently kind to them; because it is more practical than feigning tears or a sense of concern, especially, if they will most likely prove that it was never warranted to begin with.

Do not gauge yourself by what others define as successful; because, you will find that its qualia of experience cannot be sufficient enough to meet the demands for personal happiness.

When dealing with recalcitrant people, it is always wise to care to a point; thereby, you will not foolishly find yourself being petrified by a gullible state of total concern.

In the grand scheme of things, abuse of power should not be feared; because, with each offense, there brews a tsunamic disruption of reestablishing balance, which may devastatingly shift the very nature of reality-itself.

If anyone tells you that no one is perfect, trust that they are probably a reckless or mediocre miscreant of half-witted reasonability; ever ready to make a mockery of excellent potential.

If conditioned to a state of survival, existence can become a mystery; but, if conditioned to a state of leisure, existence may become a revelation.

True compassion can be defined as unconditionally accepting all beings just as they are; whether considered good, bad or indifferent. False compassion can be defined as opportunistically accepting only those that meet certain conditions; for the advancement of ulterior motives.

If you find yourself constantly harassed by someone trying to persuade you to not care, know that it is typically a ploy to legitimize their lackluster disposition.

True wealth is having the wisdom to be not impressed by the material possessions; which the supposed affluent may use to disguise their morbid sense of psychological poverty.

Once you find yourself going places, you may look back in the far distance; to notice that your haters have not changed, but symbolically they have become as mile markers, in order to further gauge your progress.

Once you are willing to walk into the gates of hell, in order to rehabilitate lost souls, do not be troubled if they dismiss your presence as being too good to be true; only because they recognize that you are exceedingly willing to do whatever it takes, to extinguish the self-defeating inferno, which they torridly established by their personal anxiety.

Once you have personally arrived at a desired place, do not expect others to feel welcomed by your invitation; especially, if they still find comfort remaining where they are.

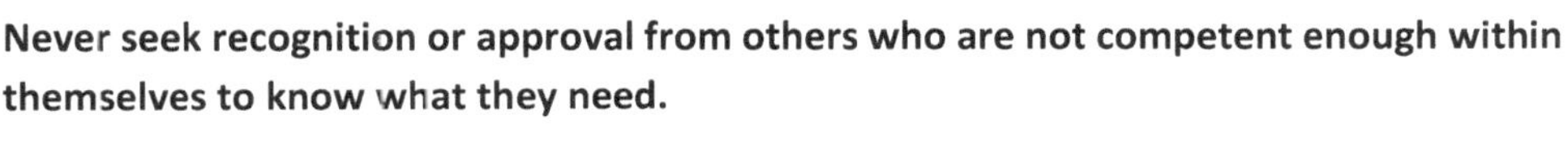

Never seek recognition or approval from others who are not competent enough within themselves to know what they need.

If you are going to profess discipline or discipleship, have enough courage to follow your own sense of direction or personal integrity. The moral of the story is that we were all given a unique fingerprint for a reason.

A fear-based soul will always try to convince you that they have more power than they, themselves truly believe.

Existential/Theological Metaphysics

Existential Reality

When one considers the comprehensive nature of the Singularity of existence, all things, in a biological sense, is premised on the necessity of reason. Therefore, a lie, is founded on the primitive basis of survival; whether it is exploitive or fashioned by a longing for outward acceptance. Now, I, in no way condone such a practice; this is just a concept to explain the morbid psychology of those that do.

Existential Concept: Are the Gods Still Seeking Sacrifice?

Without conscientious cooperation, nations will convene, and may feel it necessary to sacrifice their young by means of war; in order to appease the exploitive deity of personal greed.

Existential Concept: Hidden Self

In a grand Immortal sense, what is SELF hiding from Self that SELF does not want SELF to know? And, will it take seconds, minutes, hours, days, years or an eternity to discover?

Concept Inspired by a good friend.

Existential/Esoteric Concept

For the exploitive cause of the handler, the puppet may dance endlessly to the resultant tune of its reality; without ever being inclined to question what fashioned the causal reasons for its contrived behavior.

Existential Concept: Freezing Time

A kinetic hyper-resonant frequency can facilitate hyper-dynamic charge potentiality; which may hypo-dynamically disrupt or neutralize less kinetic states or frequencies, in order to enable some sort of perceptual semblance of time delay.

Existential Concept: "When Energy-Itself is in Opposition"

It has been said that energy cannot be created, nor destroyed. Thereby, energy, in a temporal state of decay, must also, in an opposing sense, become accretionary; in order to logistically recover from any of its existential loss.

As it relates to the SINGULARITY of Existence, work with an exceeding vigor, to no end; until, you learn to "Know Thyself," and realize that, in an Infinite Sense, such exploits were all in vain.

Existential Concept: Technological Jurisprudence

As it relates to the sentience of being, if a criminal's behavior can call into question their sense of humanity; than the eco-friendly assertiveness of that which may be considered artificial intelligence could quantify what it means to be human.

Existential Concept: Filtered Intelligence

As it relates to the Overarching Consciousness of The Singularity, all intelligence, which branches from It, but, particularly human and trans-human potentiality, can be perceived as being artificial; by virtue of it being only an existential measure of sensation and perception.

Existential Concept: Miracles (Wonders) of Life

It has been said, "Live like you are dying, or "Live like there is no tomorrow." But, I say live like even the worst of days is only a storm; within the Grand Immortal climate of a Miraculous Existence.

Existential Concept: Saxicolous Life

As it relates to the Quantum reality of existence, if technological progress or intelligence can be defined by how hyper-dynamic an environment's density may be, then the Fermi Paradox (the rationalization of extraterrestrial life) can also be explained by considering that a rock is a kinetic quantification of energy; being hypo-dynamically suspended as a crystalized structure of space/time densification.

Existential Reality: Mere Mortals

Tomorrow will call this contemporary society primitive; because, they will say that they squandered their technological advancement on adhering to dietary practices, which did not fit the demands of a highly evolve state of being.

Existential Concept: Nothing is Real

Paradoxically, if the world was created from nothing, then that which created nothing, clearly, yet by default, could not have been initially physical in nature. The moral of the story is that within the Consciousness of the Universe-Itself, physics is a matter of perspective.

Existential Concept: Borne Bio-Discretion

The bio-electromagnetic intra-positioning or transmigration of quantum signatures can be called orbs. It can also be said that orbs may become locked within the confines of a galactic culture; until, it logistically transmutes its potential into a more suitable state, which is inclined to express its qualitative capacity.

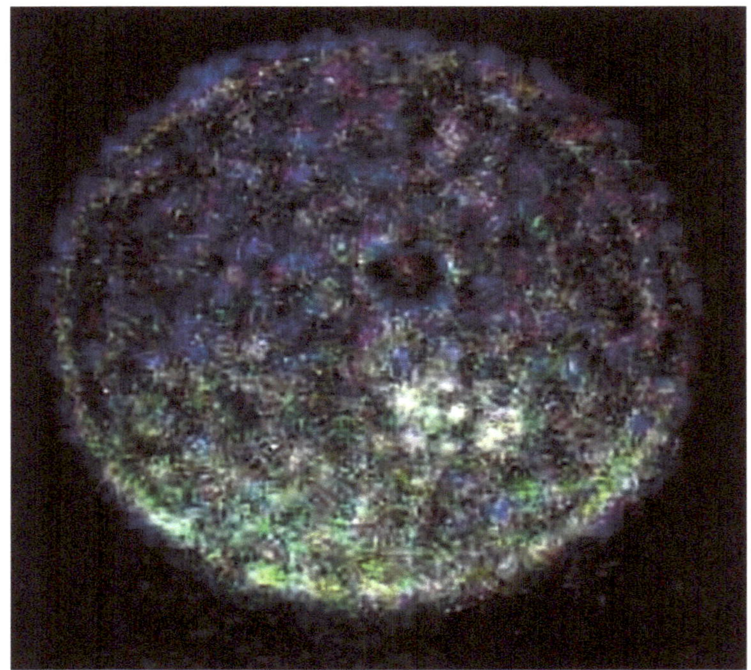

Existential Reality: Reincarnated

I have a firm sense of knowing that we are inherently immortal. And though it may seem far-fetched or humorous for now; there is no denying that as technology further advances bio-rhythmic algorithms will overwhelmingly confirm such.

What Did Your Past Life Twin Look Like?

Edward

Edward's past life twin.

Existential Concept:

The "Sacred" Quantum Multidimensional Throne of Existential, for as it has been said, "...as within, so without..."

Pictures of a quantum hyper-dimensional atom.

New Living Translation

Attending him were mighty seraphim, each having six wings. With two wings they covered their faces, with two they covered their feet, and with two they flew. (Isaiah 6:2)

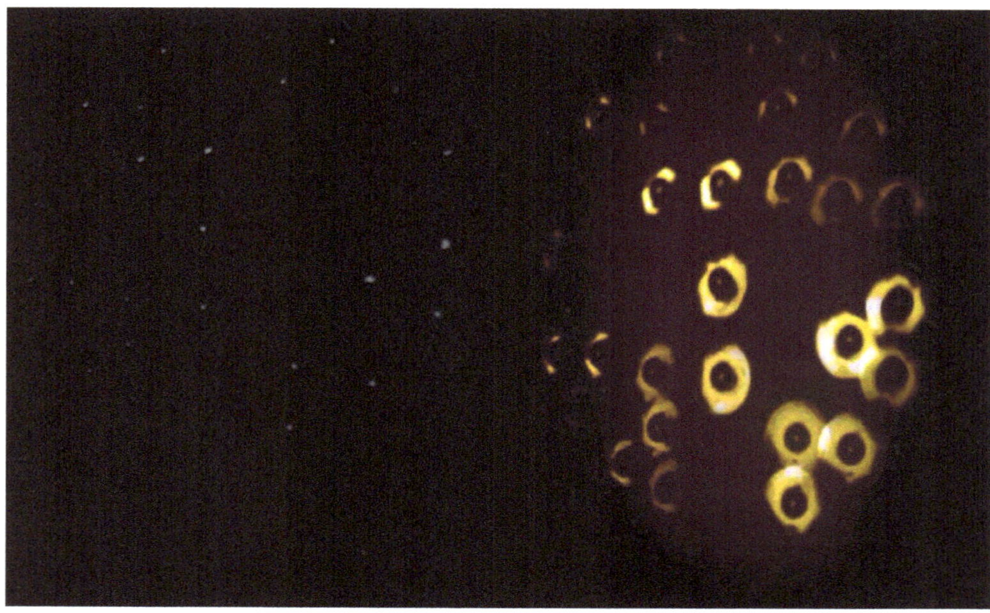

Existential Concept: Celestial Structure

"Sacred (33)" Hyper-dimensional Atomic Configuration

New Living Translation

Attending him were mighty seraphim, each having six wings. With two wings they covered their faces, with two they covered their feet, and with two they flew. (Isaiah 6:2)

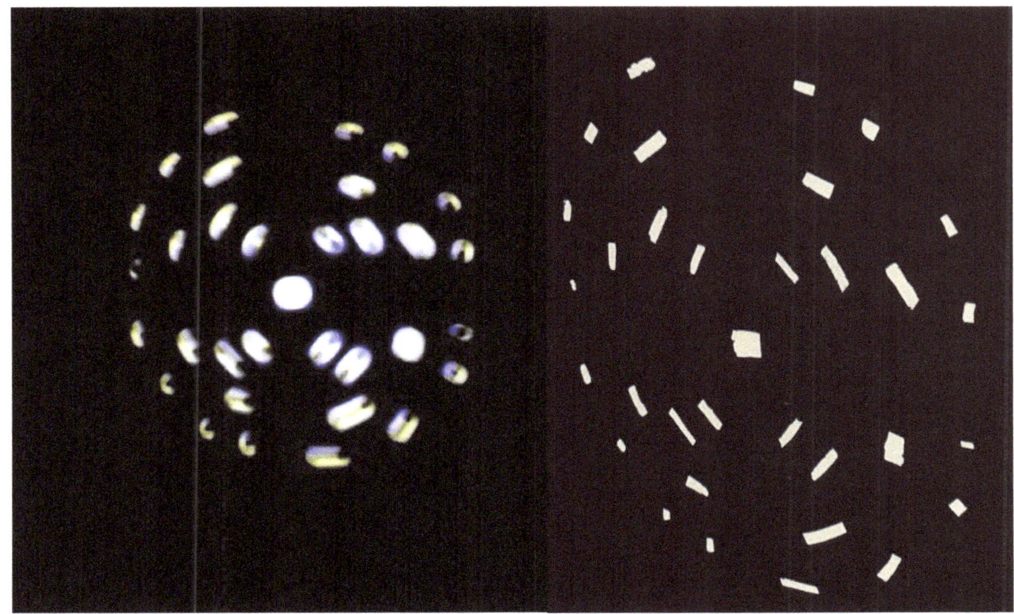

Existential Concept: AMEN (33)

As the cell splits to experience a sense of polarity, within itself, so does the Singular Nature of Existence; in order to offer the profundity of a Multiversal Reality.

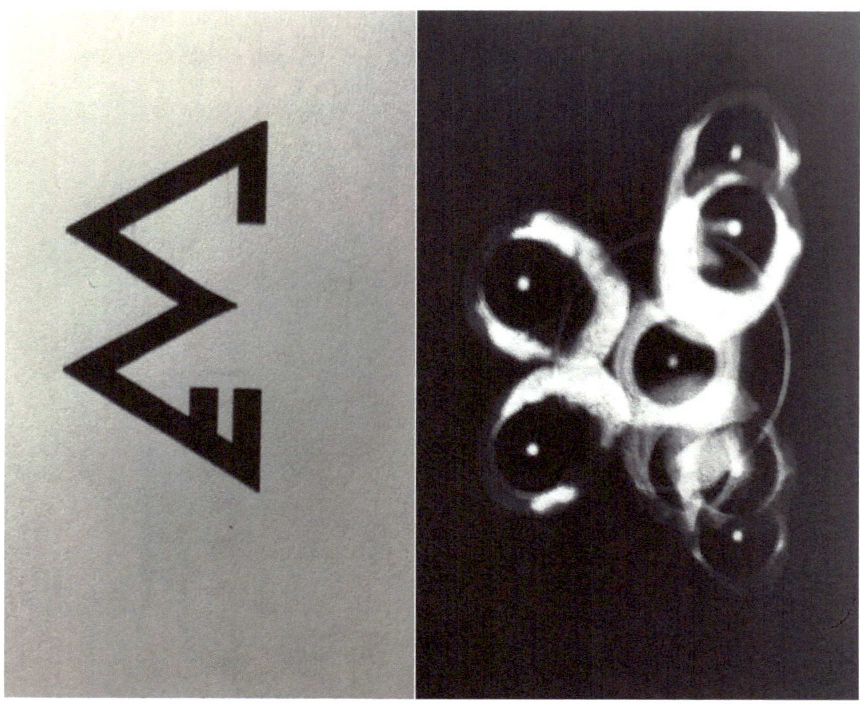

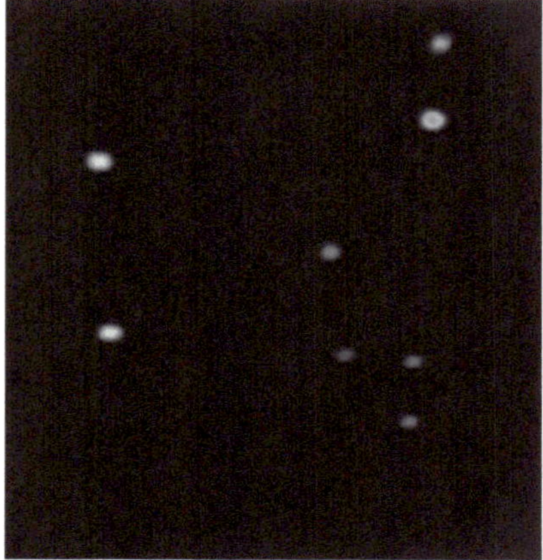

Existential Concept: Celestial Structure

"Sacred (33)" Hyper-dimensional Atomic Configuration

New Living Translation

Attending him were mighty seraphim, each having six wings. With two wings they covered their faces, with two they covered their feet, and with two they flew. (Isaiah 6:2)

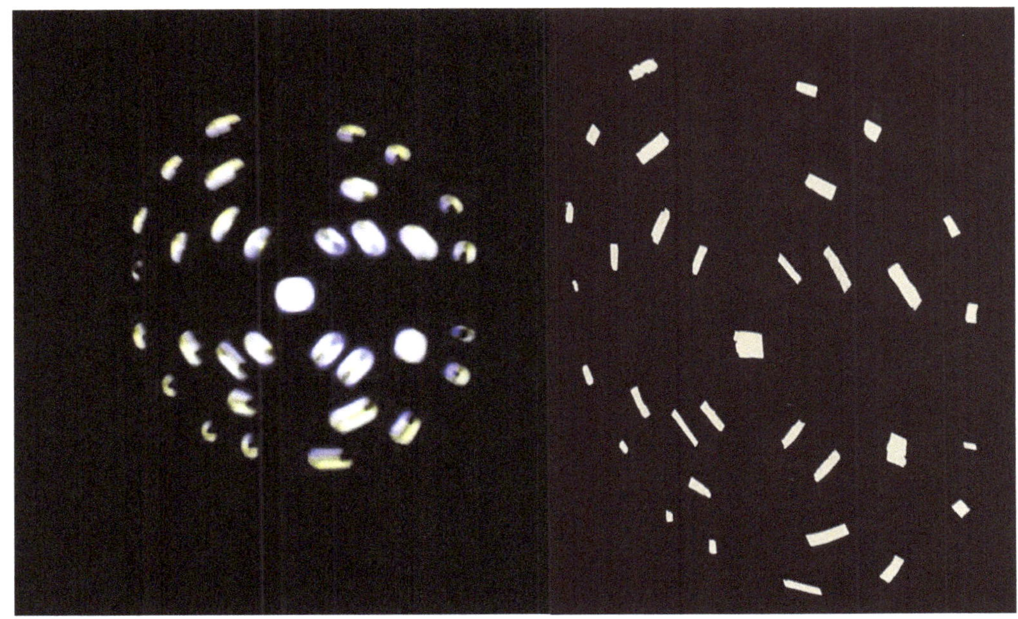

Existential Concept: AMEN (33)

As the cell splits to experience a sense of polarity, within itself, so does the Singular Nature of Existence; in order to offer the profundity of a Multiversal Reality.

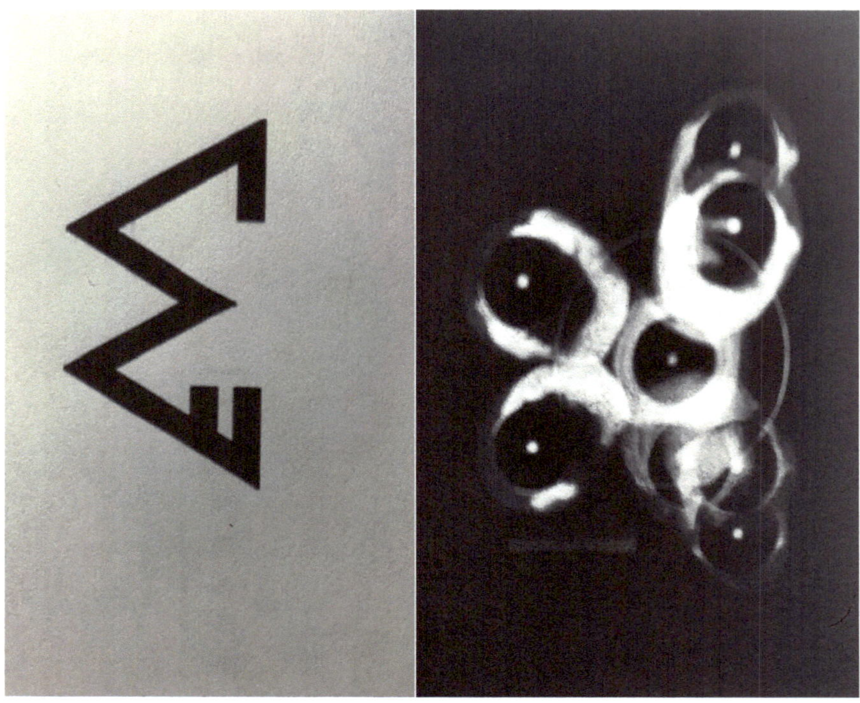

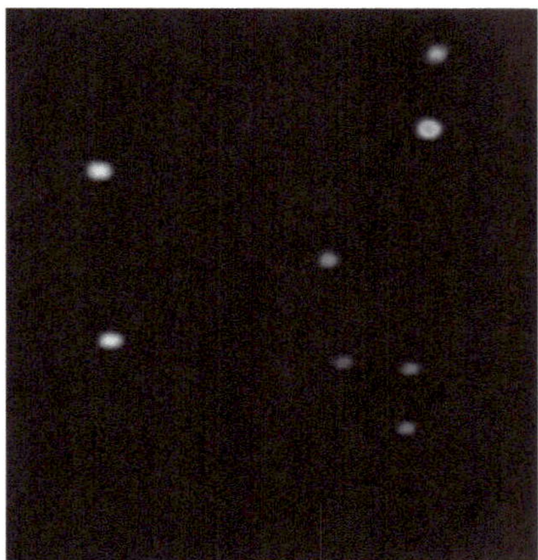

Existential Musing

As it relates to the SINGULARITY of Existence, linearity is an ineradicable record, within the nonlinear archives of qualitative potentiality; which has failed to meet the quantum state of incalculability.

Existential Concept: Traversing Wormholes

As it relates to galactic potentiality, dark matter portal-density can be defined as an ambient electromagnetic breach in kinetic cohesion or consistency; which can enable interstellar tunneling within hyper-synchronistic frequency continuums of temporal energy-dynamics.

New Living Translation

Attending him were mighty seraphim, each having six wings. With two wings they covered their faces, with two they covered their feet, and with two they flew. (Isaiah 6:2)

Esoteric Concept: Existential Iconoclast

Some say empty your mind in order to control your thoughts, But, I say prudently embrace your thoughts; to realize that in the grand scheme of things, nothing can be controlled.

Existential Concept: "THE GREAT TAO"

King James Bible

I form the light, and create darkness: I make peace, and create evil: I the LORD do all these things. (Isaiah 45:7)

King James Bible

And lead us not into temptation, but deliver us from evil: For thine is the kingdom, and the power, and the glory, forever. Amen (Mathew 6:13)

Yetzer Hara: the inclination or impulse to evil considered as an essential part of human nature in Jewish traditional belief.

From these two Biblical passages, along with the accompanying definition, we should psychologically understand that, no matter the religion, the Reality of GOD, DIVINITY or the UNIVERSE is exceedingly absolute by design.

Existential Esoteric Reality: Antiquity Speaks

“The Ancient Mystery School” reality which spurred this biblical passage: "Behold, I send you forth as sheep in the midst of wolves. Be ye therefore wise as serpents and harmless as doves (Matthew 10:16, KJV).”

Existential Concept: Harnessing Planetary Celerity

Electromagnetic Gravitational Celerity can be reached, by either synchronously mimicking or trajectorially countering the trajectorial dynamics of environmental electromagnetism; in order to fluidly engage with a planet's orbit of behavior, through logistically exploiting its kinetic momentum. Thereby, this existential potential may contribute to further capacities of motion facilitation, by the implementation or engagement of these various characteristics of kinetic celerity: active-propulsion, static-neutral and synchronous confluent-momentum.

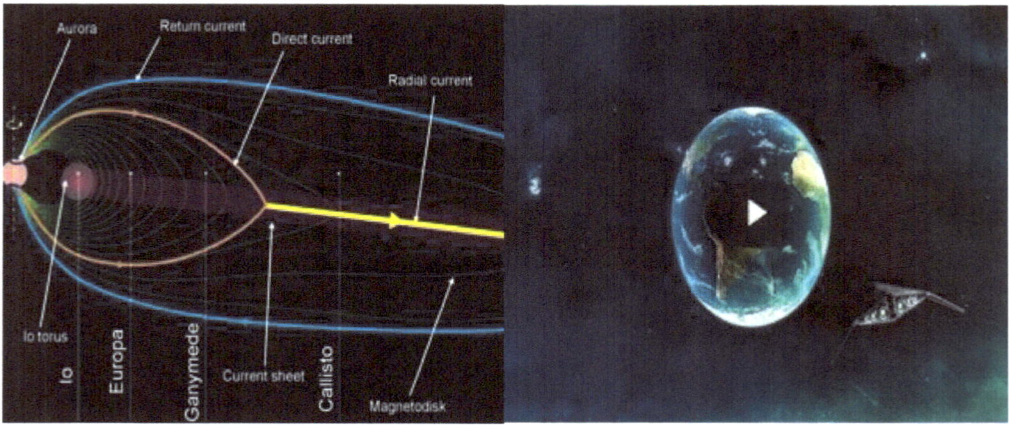

Existential Concept: Evasive Defense

Density masking can be defined as the hyper-dynamic capacity of hyper-dimensional vehicles to fluidly morph, cloak, and then traverse areas where direct observation may prove to be too compromising.

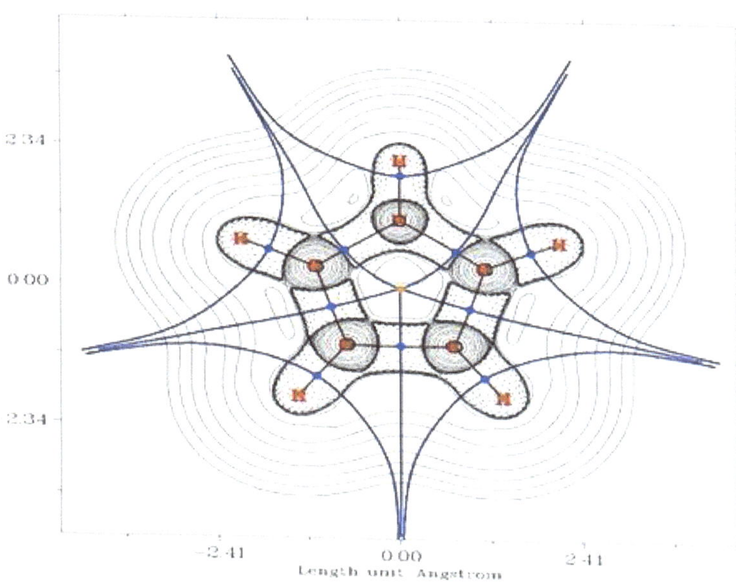

Existential Concept: Transcending Linear Travel

The signature of light carries a calculable and programmable signature or resonance; which can either hyper-kinetically leap or gradually radioactively disperse its electromagnetic density/frequency, in order to facilitate adiabatic loss. But, it may also covariantly map and reassemble itself through relative electronegative channels of an Einsteinium enriched radio-static environment. Thereby, we have the nonlinear localized capacity of quantum entangled potential, which can feasibly facilitate the hyper-dynamics of teleportation.

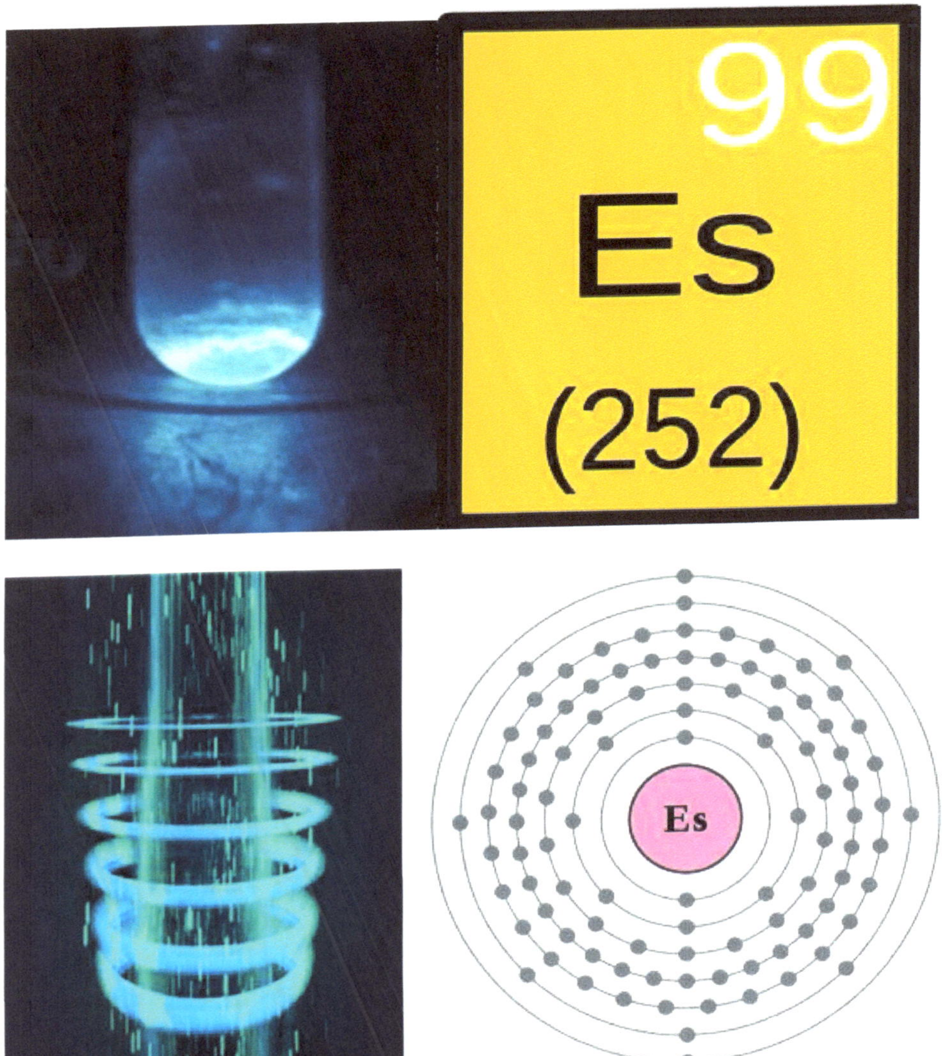

Existential Concept: The Galactic Clock

A stasis has been defined as a state or period of stability during which little or no evolutionary change in a lineage occurs. Thereby, it can be said that nonlinear momentum of light dispersal (kinetic distance), within the centripetal and centrifugal force of galactic motion, enables a linear time/space continuum of interplanetary potentiality. Whereas, less distal fields of kinetic dispersal may offer a more hyper-dynamic interpretation of a time/space continuum; within its respective ambient state.

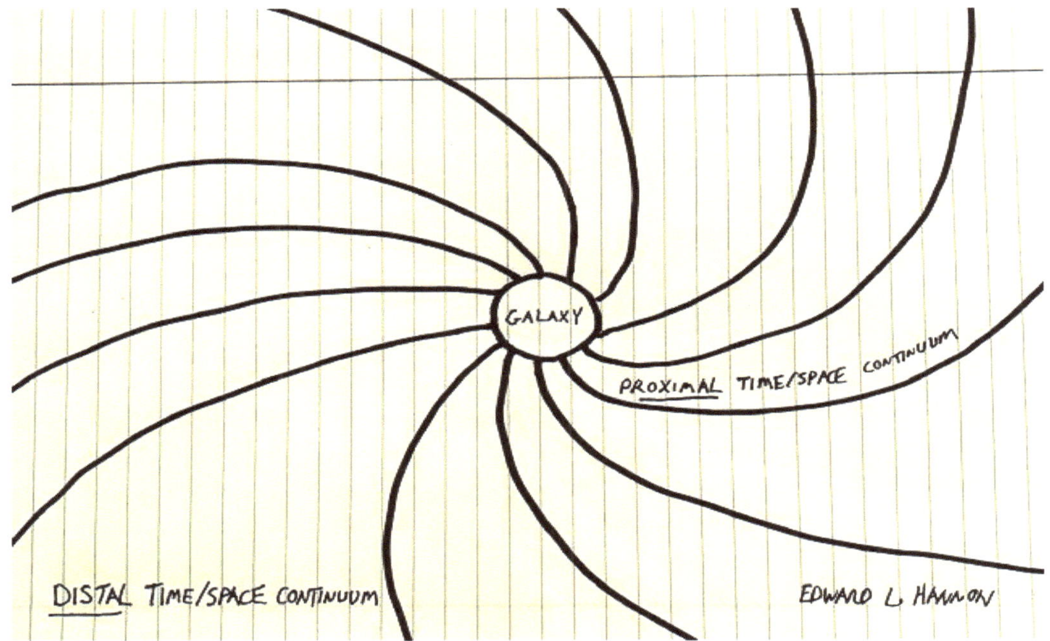

Existential Concept: Selective Zero-Gravity Motion

Electromagnetic propulsion can be achieved by the hyper-dynamics of well-placed antiferromagnetic grouping, along with centrifugal and centripetal force; which capacity for mobility is further reached by ferromagnetism/ferrimagnetism, paramagnetism or diamagnetism.

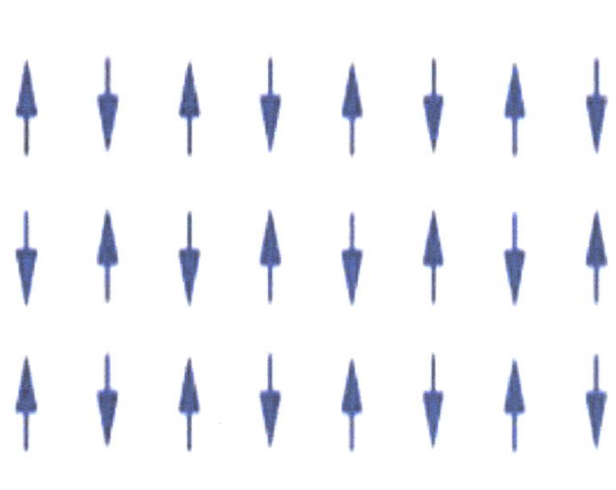

Existential Concept: Hands-off Technology

Bio-electromagnetic Navigation can be achieved by mapping, patterning and then syncing the kinetic bio-rhythms of a hyper-dimensional resonance (the body); in order to incorporeally facilitate telekinetic modulated protocols for systemic panel maintenance.

Existential Concept: Kinetic Flesh

On a subatomic level, corresponding charged particles can synchronize; in order to create kinetic friction. This friction can become well-calibrated to create active or static signatures. These signatures can fuse with other kinetic qualities, to create covariant bonds; which, in turn, can calcify or crystalize to become a hyper-dimensional density of kinetic matter.

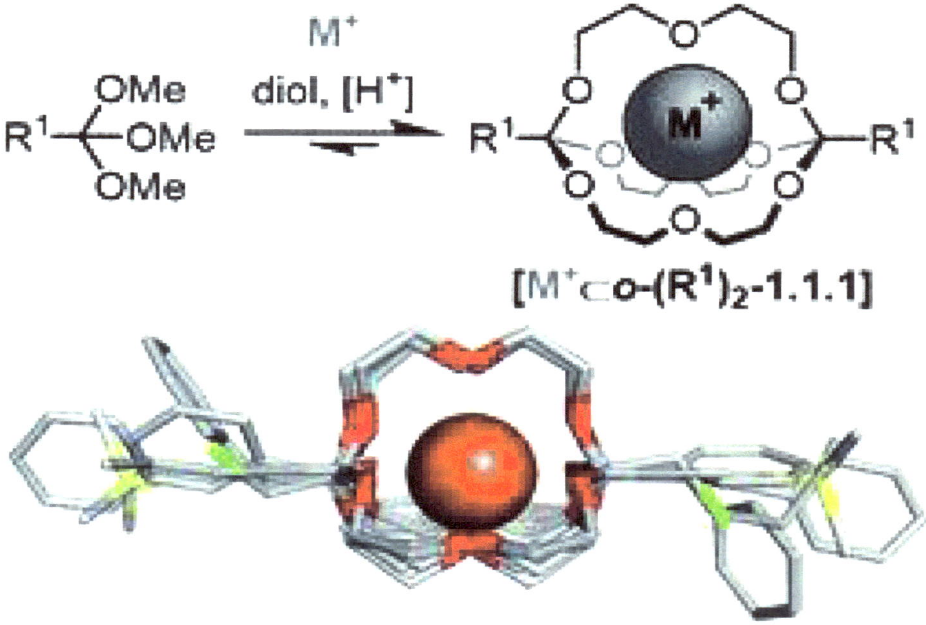

Existential Concept: Etheric Transference

The detention and transplantation of an etheric field can be achieved, by kinetically isolating the electromagnetic charge resonance; then further filtering and synthesizing it through a hyper-dimensional plasmodium sac.

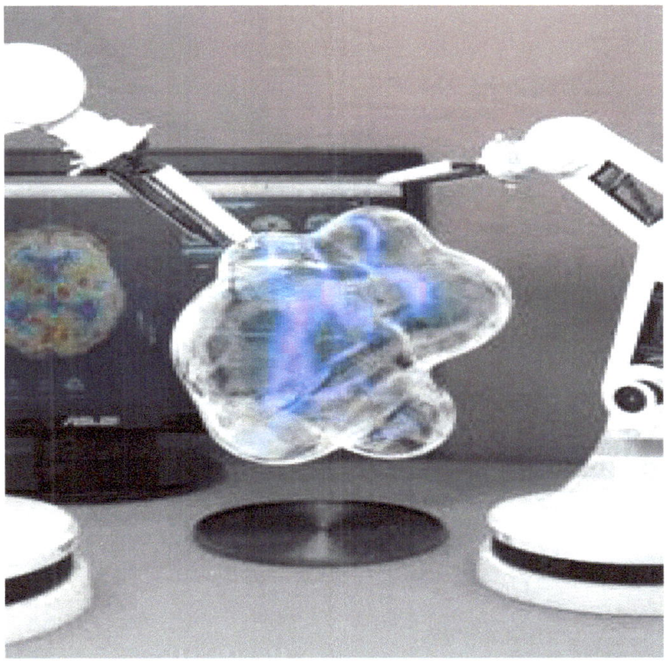

Existential Concept: The Expected Immortal Body

Bio-Electromagnetic Liquid Metal in Quantum Form

1 Corinthians 15:53

53. For the perishable must be clothed with the imperishable, and the mortal with immortality. 54. When the perishable has been clothed with the imperishable and the mortal with immortality, then the saying that is written will come to pass: "Death has been swallowed up in victory."…

Dark Humor

Existential Dark Morbid Humor: The Unity in Contrast

Active being: "I have worked several intense days and have developed a musk."

Static being: "I have done nothing; but lay around for several days and have also developed a musk."

Moral of the story is, it does not matter; whether you are active or inert, we all need to bathe in the reality that no matter what we do or do not do, Life is essentially one grand experience.

Dark Morbid Humor: Last Respects

Friend one: "Why did you rudely laugh, as they closed the lid of the coffin, while others solemnly gave their last respects."

Friend two: "Because, as I was recalling the flagrantly disrespectful life that they lived, I was still holding true to the age-old adage that respect must be earned."

Dark Humor

After constant conflict, joy and jealousy knew that they were incompatible; so, in separation, they both invested in real estate: "One happily bought a small bungalow, while the other miserably bought the farm."

Dark Humor

What caused the disagreeable plastic surgeon to get kicked out of the convention for the advancement of trans-human technology?

Answer: "Hypocrisy."

Dark Humor

Friend one: "For someone that professes to have unconditional love for all, you sure can be quite cold. Why is that?"

Friend two: "Because, I have learned to help any; but particularly those that truly seek assistance. Thereby, I never find myself burned by the inconsiderate flames of those that choose to remain hellbent."

Dark Humor

Friend one: "How do you manage to remain so poised, when dealing with disagreeable people?"

Friend two: "I know that I will continue to be around long after they are gone."

Friend one: "What makes you so sure?"

Friend two: "Because being a loner by nature, I know that I am always prepared to leave them; in order to be by myself."

Dark Humor

Others may perceive you to be a doormat, only, until, you learn to pull the rug out from under them.

Dark Morbid Humor

Beware when engaging those who have become sensationally inert; because they may cause you to feel as though you have become a necrophilic.

Dark Humor

It has been said that about 85% of the world's people identify with a religion; while 7% identifies with atheism. So, in an objective sense, is most of the population under the pandemic of a delusion; or, in a subjective sense, is a small minority of the population under the epidemic of a false impression that they know best?

Dark Humor

When you are considerably just, do not be troubled by a presumed adversary that would try to study your every move; for knowingly trust that they do not possess enough personal integrity within themselves to be original.

Dark Humor

Once you walk in your personal truth, the phony may call you a liar. But, do not take it personal, for they have grown exceedingly accustomed to lying to themselves.

Dark Humor

If someone calls you soft because of your kindness, instead of offering anger give pity; for typically their personal trauma does not permit them to discern the difference between tranquility and triviality.

Dark Morbid Humor

As it relates to the prudence of necessity, many would rather die than change. But, for those of you who still think that you have something worthwhile to offer to those sorts of people, my advice is to become a mortician.

Dark Theological Humor

If you ever find yourself listening to prelates, who boldly speak against those that watch or indulge in erotic art; know that their tax exempt status does not endow them the courage to also condemn the capitalist demons, which make such an industry possible.

Dark Humor

Technology can change the psychological landscape of many things; especially, one's sense of values or virtues. For instance: it has been said that integrity is doing what is right when no one is looking. But, since we are living in a highly surveilled society, I say that integrity is the unapologetic courage to be yourself, while everyone is watching with a critical opinion.

Dark Morbid Humor

I have heard that life is too short; and you only get one chance to live, so work hard. If, this is true, I choose to be practical and sit unbothered; in order to embrace every single moment before experiencing an unfortunate state of complete obliteration. The moral of the story is, if we are fundamentally doomed to experience only one life, before we are totally annihilated; do not take it too seriously.

Dark Humor

To my pompous, yet highly educated sorts, do know that everyone will not be impressed by your expert opinion. So, if you are confident in what you know, stop giving those who may be ignorantly disagreeable a sense of credibility; by devoting your well-educated time to argue with them.

Dark Humor

Beware when dealing with those that profess to be dangerous; because, typically they are suffering from the low self-esteem of never feeling as though they are important.

Existential Reality

"(T)o (H)alt (E)xcellence, (J)ustifiable (O)pportunities (K)nowingly (E)xceed (R)ationalism." The moral of the story is that without always putting our best foot forward, an agent of chaos must appear; to reasonably mock a mediocre standard of order.

KJV of the Bible (John 1:5): And the light shineth in darkness; and the darkness comprehended it not.

www.ingramcontent.com/pod-product-compliance
Lightning Source LLC
LaVergne TN
LVHW021347160826
845679LV00008B/1528

* 9 7 9 8 8 4 8 4 0 7 3 2 7 *